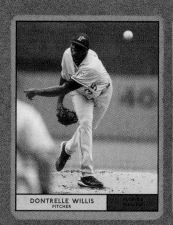
DONTRELLE WILLIS
PITCHER
FLORIDA MARLINS

GARY SHEFFIELD
RIGHT FIELDER
FLORIDA MARLINS

THE STORY OF THE **FLORIDA MARLINS**

Published by Creative Education
P.O. Box 227, Mankato, Minnesota 56002
Creative Education is an imprint of The Creative Company
www.thecreativecompany.us

Design and production by Blue Design
Art direction by Rita Marshall
Printed by Corporate Graphics in the United States of America

Photographs by Getty Images (Joel Auerbach, Al Bello, Lisa Blumenfeld, Angelo Cavalli, Tom DiPace/
Sports Illustrated, Stephen Dunn, Elsa, Steve Green/MLB Photos, Jeff Haynes/AFP, Jed Jacobsohn, Nick
Laham, Mitchell Layton, Mitchell Layton/MLB Photos, Ronald C. Modra/Sports Imagery, Doug Pensinger,
Rich Pilling/MLB Photos, Eliot J. Schechter, Ezra Shaw, Don Smith/MLB Photos, Jamie Squire, Matthew
Stockman, Rhona Wise/AFP, Mike Zarrilli)

Library of Congress Cataloging-in-Publication Data

Gilbert, Sara.
The story of the Florida Marlins / by Sara Gilbert.
p. cm. — (Baseball: the great American game)
Includes index.
Summary: The history of the Florida Marlins professional baseball team from its inaugural 1993 season to
today, spotlighting the team's greatest players and most memorable moments.
ISBN 978-1-60818-041-7
1. Florida Marlins (Baseball team)—History—Juvenile literature. I. Title. II. Series.

GV875.F56G55 2011
796.357'6409759381—dc22   2010024398

CPSIA: 110310 PO1381

First Edition
9 8 7 6 5 4 3 2 1

Page 3: Shortstop Edgar Renteria
Page 4: Infielder Jorge Cantu

BASEBALL: THE GREAT AMERICAN GAME

THE STORY OF THE
FLORIDA MARLINS

CREATIVE EDUCATION

CONTENTS

FRESH FISH

On almost any given day, the sun is likely to shine in Miami, Florida. The National Weather Service reports that on average, 70 percent of the daylight hours in Miami are sunny. Combine that with the fact that average temperatures are in the 70s and 80s all year long, and it's understandable why Miami, situated near the southeastern tip of the Florida peninsula, is one of the most popular vacation spots in the United States. The beaches are a beautiful place to play, and the Atlantic Ocean is a great place for deep-sea fishing. There are endless sporting events as well; the city hosts both Indy and NASCAR races and is home to several professional sports teams—even a National Hockey League franchise, the Florida Panthers.

Miami's climate, however, is better suited to baseball than hockey. For decades, the city has hosted spring training facilities for several Major League Baseball teams, which appreciate the region's beautiful winter weather. But since 1993, it has also been home to a team of its own: the Florida Marlins, which joined the National League (NL) as an

Summer never seems to end in Miami, where palm trees wave year-round amid daytime temperatures that rarely dip much below 70 degrees.

PITCHER · DONTRELLE WILLIS

Dontrelle Willis, nicknamed "D-Train," was a minor-leaguer with the Chicago Cubs when he was traded to the Marlins in 2002. At first, Willis, capable of throwing heat approaching 100 miles per hour, attempted to smooth out his herky-jerky delivery style, but then he realized that his unusual method aided in his deception of batters. The enthusiasm and broad smile Willis frequently exhibited on the field endeared him to Marlins fans, as did his uncommonly good batting ability. In June 2006, the hard-throwing lefty collected his 50th career win, moving him past A. J. Burnett on the Marlins' all-time victories list.

DONTRELLE WILLIS
PITCHER

STATS

Marlins seasons: 2003–07

Height: 6-foot-4

Weight: 215

• 2003 NL Rookie of the Year

• 2-time All-Star

• First Marlins pitcher to win 20 games in a season (2005)

• 4.12 career ERA

expansion team that year. Wayne Huizenga, who owned the Blockbuster Video corporation as well as the Miami Dolphins football team, was granted franchise rights and took it upon himself to name the new team. "I chose Marlins," said Huizenga, a deep-sea fisherman, "because the fish is a fierce fighting adversary that tests your mettle."

Huizenga moved his new Marlins into Miami's Joe Robbie Stadium, which was also the home of the Dolphins. Although the open-air stadium was converted to accommodate the baseball team and the palm-tree-landscaped venue was beautiful, few modifications could lessen the extreme heat of summer days or the thunderstorms that plagued Miami at night. "Pick up the park and move it 500 miles north," quipped sportswriter Jeff Merron, "and you've got a real winner." Even in the midst of such uncomfortable conditions, however, Florida fans fell in love with the team, snapping up season tickets before the club ever took the field.

The Marlins' first player acquisitions included hustling catcher Benito Santiago, pitcher Bryan Harvey, and hard-hitting outfielder Jeff Conine. On April 5, 1993, a crowd of 42,334 watched the Marlins win their first regular-season game, 6–3, over the Los Angeles Dodgers. Conine quickly became a fan favorite, hitting .292 and driving in 79 runs as Florida posted a 64–98 record in its inaugural season.

The brawny Conine was joined in midseason by slugger Gary Sheffield, a Florida native who arrived via a trade with the San Diego Padres. Sheffield led the Marlins' offense in 1994 by slamming 27 home runs in just 87 games. With his offensive power, the "Fighting Fish," as the Marlins became known, posted a 51–64 record during the strike-shortened 1994 season. Hurler Robb Nen demonstrated his future All-Star form by saving 15 games, while fleet young center fielder Chuck Carr swiped 32 bases. Marlins manager Rene Lachemann saw these performances as reason for optimism. "I like the direction we are headed," he told reporters.

Due to the lingering players' strike, the 1995 season got off to a late start, but once it did, the Marlins faithful witnessed even greater fireworks. Fans were awed by a run of 14 straight home wins at Joe Robbie Stadium in July. Catcher Charles Johnson, a former All-American from the nearby University of Miami, put on a defensive clinic behind the plate, his quick hands and cannon arm stopping many would-be base stealers dead in their tracks. And with veteran third baseman Terry Pendleton wielding a sure glove at the hot corner, the young Marlins ended their third year with a respectable 67–76 record.

JEFF CONINE

A TEAL MONSTER AND MORE

The Marlins' ballpark was originally called Joe Robbie Stadium, then Pro Player Stadium, then Dolphin Stadium. In 2009, after a $250-million renovation, it became known as Sun Life Stadium. It is often compared to Fenway Park in Boston, as both stadiums contain notoriously tall left-field walls and hazardous nooks and crannies in the outfield fence that create tough bounces for outfielders. Florida's wall is nicknamed "The Teal Monster" as a nod to Fenway's famous "Green Monster." Other quirks abound in the park. A clock atop the center-field wall sometimes robs hitters of home runs. A notch in deep center field creates a mysterious area known as the "Bermuda Triangle," where players can hit the ball 433 feet without it ever leaving the park, leading to frequent triples. Because of Miami's summer heat, which "cools" to a sticky 85 °F on August nights, Sun Life Stadium is not always a ballpark fans want to visit. But the stadium does get top ratings from visitors for its hot dogs and also offers hearty local fare, such as Cuban sandwiches and conch fritters. Such concessions will likely follow the Marlins to their new state-of-the-art stadium, which was expected to be completed in time for the 2012 season.

CATCHER • CHARLES JOHNSON

Florida native Charles "Chuck" Johnson was born and raised in Fort Pierce and attended the University of Miami. He was the starting catcher on the U.S. baseball team in the 1992 Summer Olympic Games and then joined the Marlins via the first round of the 1992 amateur draft. Johnson got a key base hit during the pivotal Game 7 of the 1997 World Series, driving home outfielder Moises Alou to tie the game. Johnson left Florida in 1998 but returned three seasons later. During the 2001 season, he donated $100 to charity each time he threw out a base stealer.

STATS

Marlins seasons: 1994–98, 2001–02

Height: 6-foot-2

Weight: 215

• 2-time All-Star

• 4-time Gold Glove winner

• 167 career HR

• 570 career RBI

CHARLES JOHNSON
CATCHER

FLORIDA
MARLINS

FIRST BASEMAN · DERREK LEE

Derrek Lee came by his baseball ability naturally, being the son of Leon Lee and the nephew of Leron Lee, both of whom played for the Lotte Orions baseball team in Kawasaki, Japan. Lee was the total package of power, speed, and defensive ability. He was a giant at first base, standing 6-foot-5, yet he showed impressive fielding range and was surprisingly nimble around the bag. Lee was born in California but learned to respect the game of baseball watching his father play in Japan. He left the Marlins in 2003, when he signed with the Chicago Cubs.

STATS

Marlins seasons: 1998–2003

Height: 6-foot-5

Weight: 240

- 3-time Gold Glove winner
- 2-time All-Star
- .282 career BA
- 312 career HR

DERREK LEE
FIRST BASEMAN

MARLINS

[14]

CATCHING THE BIG ONE

Prior to the 1996 season, the Marlins signed hurlers Kevin Brown and Al Leiter. The left-handed Leiter wasted no time in winning over Florida fans, striking out six batters as he fired the franchise's first no-hitter in an 11–0 whitewashing of the Colorado Rockies on May 11. However, by mid-July, the Marlins were mired in a slump, so Huizenga fired Lachemann and moved vice president John Boles onto the bench in an effort to spark the team. The move seemed to help, and the Marlins finished the season with an 80–82 mark, third in the NL Eastern Division.

Boles returned to the Marlins' front office in 1997 when former Pittsburgh Pirates skipper Jim Leyland was hired as the third Florida manager. Leyland's lineup included several new additions, such as burly third baseman Bobby Bonilla, pitcher Alex Fernandez, and outfielder Moises Alou. With a combined total of 97 home runs from Bonilla, Alou, Johnson, Conine, and Sheffield and 17, 16, and 11 wins from Fernandez, Brown, and Leiter, respectively, the Marlins blazed to

FIRST SPLASH

The front-page headlines shouted "Play Ball" and "Batter Up," words Florida sports fans had been longing to hear for years. The Florida Marlins made their major-league debut on April 5, 1993, against the Los Angeles Dodgers, a team that was founded in 1890. Under sunny Florida skies, a festive atmosphere pervaded Joe Robbie Stadium, including the world-renowned Florida A&M marching band and tributes to the men responsible for giving baseball a summer home in the fourth-largest state in the country. Hall of Fame outfielder Joe DiMaggio, then age 78, tossed out the ceremonial first pitch. Next, 45-year-old Charlie Hough, who grew up near Miami, took the mound for the expansion Marlins, and a crowd of 42,334 fans stood and cheered his first pitch. "I'll never forget it," said Hough. "All those years I watched baseball come in the spring and then leave." The crowd roared again when Hough struck out the first two batters with his famous knuckleballs in a 1-2-3 first inning. Hough pitched solidly until reliever Bryan Harvey eventually took over for the save in the 6–3 Florida win. At the final out, in a scene more befitting an October playoff game than an opening day contest, leaping, shouting Marlins players ran onto the field to celebrate the historic victory.

a 92–70 season finish—just behind the Atlanta Braves in the NL East race. Although they missed the division championship, the Marlins captured the NL Wild Card berth into the playoffs.

In their first postseason, the Marlins met the San Francisco Giants in the NL Division Series (NLDS). Incredibly, the underdog Marlins proved themselves the more unflappable team in the playoffs. Clutch hits from Alou and shortstop Edgar Renteria helped them win Games 1 and 2. In Game 3, speedy center fielder Devon White slugged a sixth-inning grand slam to propel Florida to a 6–2 victory, wrapping up a three-game sweep of the Giants. "This is great," White said afterward, "but we have another hill to climb."

The NL Championship Series (NLCS) pitted the Marlins against their division rivals, the Braves. Brown put forth stellar pitching performances in Games 1 and 6, and Cuban-born rookie Livan Hernandez earned the series Most Valuable Player (MVP) award by winning two games in dominant style. The Marlins toppled the Braves in six games, moving on to face the Cleveland Indians in the 1997 World Series.

Kevin Brown spent only two seasons in Florida, but they were two of the best years of his career. In 1996, he narrowly missed winning the Cy Young Award as the NL's best pitcher, and in 1997, he threw a one-hitter and a no-hitter for the Marlins.

SECOND BASEMAN · LUIS CASTILLO

Castillo's trademark was the "slap and dash" game, as he often worked deep pitch counts and then showed off wicked foot speed after making contact at the plate. An excellent bunter, he frequently ranked among the league's leaders in infield hits, and even though he was a natural right-handed hitter, he could bat left as well. Castillo put together a 35-game hitting streak in 2002, tied for the longest ever by a second baseman. On the defensive side, Castillo was a dynamo in the field and boasted one of the strongest arms of any second-sacker in the game.

STATS

Marlins seasons: 1996–2005

Height: 5-foot-11

Weight: 190

• 3-time Gold Glove winner

• 3-time All-Star

• 2-time NL leader in stolen bases

• .290 career BA

LUIS CASTILLO
SECOND BASEMAN

Craig Counsell's World Series-winning run sent the Indians home dejected and turned Miami into the baseball capital of the world, if only for a short time.

In front of a rowdy crowd in Miami's newly renamed Pro Player Stadium, the Marlins captured Game 1 of the World Series by a 7–4 score, thanks largely to a three-run homer by Alou. The two teams split the first six games, forcing a deciding Game 7 in Florida. In the bottom of the ninth inning, with Florida down 2–1, Marlins second baseman Craig Counsell smacked a sacrifice fly that scored Alou from third and forced extra innings. After a scoreless 10th, the Marlins found themselves with the bases loaded and two outs in the 11th. The crowd went wild when Renteria hammered a ground ball up the middle that brought home the winning run. In one breathtaking moment, the Marlins had won a World Series faster than any other expansion team in major-league history. "What an amazing season," Leyland exclaimed. "For these guys to be the first team to ever win as a Wild Card just shows what heart they have."

REBUILDING ALREADY

y opening day of the 1998 season, the core of the Marlins' 1997 championship team was gone. Despite the fact that the team had drawn more than 500,000 fans during the postseason, Huizenga sold off most of his highest-paid players, claiming he could not sustain the large payroll. Florida fans watched in disbelief as Nen, Brown, White, and Conine were replaced by inexpensive minor-league prospects. After the season started, Bonilla and Johnson were let go, and Sheffield was traded to the Dodgers for catcher Mike Piazza, who was then dealt to the New York Mets. The dismantled team crashed and burned, falling to a lowly 54–108 finish just a year after standing atop the baseball world.

Before the start of the 1999 season, Huizenga sold the team to local businessman John Henry. Boles returned as manager, and the team rallied with new hope. A group of youngsters—including outfielders Preston Wilson and Cliff Floyd, second baseman Luis Castillo, first baseman Derrek Lee, and shortstop Alex Gonzalez—began to strut their stuff during the 64–98 season. Wilson immediately demonstrated

THIRD BASEMAN · MIKE LOWELL

Lowell was a master of the old hidden ball trick, in which an infielder mimes throwing the ball to the pitcher and then hides the ball before tagging out the fooled base runner when he takes a lead. Lowell's career was plagued by injury and illness—including cancer—but he always fought his way back onto the field. Although he often cracked jokes about his slowness, Lowell was a smart runner who made the most of his scoring chances. In 1999, the third baseman won the Tony Conigliaro Award, given to a player who has overcome a major obstacle and continued to succeed.

STATS

Marlins seasons: 1999–2005

Height: 6-foot-4

Weight: 205

• 4-time All-Star

• 2007 World Series MVP

• 2003 Silver Slugger winner

• 223 career HR

MIKE LOWELL
THIRD BASEMAN

FLORIDA
MARLINS

THE COLDEST GAME

The National Weather Service had warned World Series fans. A mass of cold, Canadian air was headed for Cleveland, Ohio, and Game 4 of the 1997 World Series. The Cleveland Indians' Jacobs Field, situated close to Lake Erie, was likely to receive a cold covering of lake effect snow. The first two games of the series had been played in sunny, 80-degree Florida, but on October 22, Marlins fans exchanged their T-shirts and sandals for earmuffs and fur-lined boots. Hot coffee became the chilly evening's preferred concession beverage. It was a tough night for both batters and pitchers, and players on both sides wore long underwear and turtlenecks, as well as gloves on their throwing hands. Several bats broke like brittle toothpicks amid the flurries, fielders and base runners had trouble keeping their footing, and batters got more of a sting when they connected with a fastball. The evening's low temperature of 38 °F, only 18 °F with the windchill, made the game the coldest ever in World Series history. As the contest ended in a 10–3 defeat for Florida, Marlins president Don Smiley said, "I love hunting ducks in October, and today was the Super Bowl of duck-hunting weather."

MARLINS

Preston Wilson earned a reputation as a feast-or-famine slugger, knocking
31 balls out of the park in 2000 but also striking out a whopping 187 times.

PRESTON WILSON

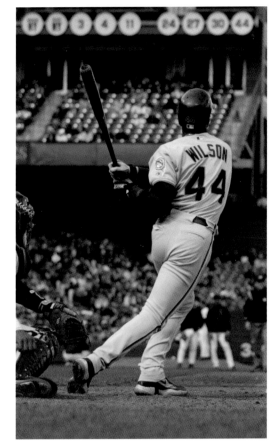

the pop in his bat by swatting 26 home runs, and
Castillo's speed netted him 50 stolen bases. The
Marlins were still in the NL East basement, but
Wilson didn't think they'd stay there for long. "The
rest of the league better get ready," he warned after
the season. "Our time is coming soon."

As a new century dawned, the Marlins' fortunes
depended upon an almost completely overhauled
pitching staff, including rookie starters Brad Penny
and A. J. Burnett and closer Antonio Alfonseca.
Alfonseca had a breakout season, leading the majors
with 45 saves, but the starting pitchers struggled. Injuries plagued the
team as well. Gonzalez suffered a strained knee, Castillo endured back
problems, and outfielder Cliff Floyd courageously played throughout
the season with a painful wrist injury. Fortunately, Castillo was well
enough to lead the league with 62 stolen bases, and Wilson slammed
a team-high 31 homers. With their help, the 2000 Marlins surged to a
third-place finish in the division with a 79–82 record.

Before the 2001 season, Florida brought World Series hero Charles
Johnson back to the team, putting a sure glove behind the plate and a

reliable bat in the lineup. Another key addition arrived in the middle of the season when former Cincinnati Reds great Tony Perez replaced John Boles as the club's manager. But the biggest headlines were prompted by rumors of contraction—or the elimination of struggling franchises— and news that the young Marlins club had been identified as a possible candidate. Adding to the unrest, team owner John Henry abruptly deserted the Marlins in order to purchase the Boston Red Sox, leaving the struggling team without an active owner until Jeffrey Loria, an art dealer and former managing partner of the Montreal Expos, finally stepped in and bought the Florida club in February 2002.

Even though Castillo produced a team-record 35-game hitting streak, Pro Player Stadium resembled a ghost town through much of the 2002 season. Signs of doom remained, despite an ultimately respectable 79–83 record, as the popular Floyd was traded away during the team's fifth straight losing season. Afterward, Wilson was dealt away for outfielder Juan Pierre, All-Star catcher Ivan "Pudge" Rodriguez was added, and the Marlins started moving in a new direction—one that emphasized pitching and speed—in hopes of becoming competitive once again. The veteran Rodriguez could see that his new team was making the right moves. "I think the 2003 season is going to be the year of the Marlins," he said.

MARLINS

One of the best defensive catchers of all time, Ivan Rodriguez was a 10-time All-Star by the time he suited up for Florida in 2003. Like a number of other star players, his time with the Marlins would prove to be brief but memorable.

SHORTSTOP · HANLEY RAMIREZ

When Hanley Ramirez finished the 2009 season with the best batting average in the NL (a franchise-record .342), Marlins owner Jeffrey Loria rewarded him with a pendant that spelled out ".342" in 394 diamonds, with a teal diamond as the decimal point. Such sparkle seemed appropriate for the young shortstop who had been a shining star for the Marlins since being named NL Rookie of the Year in 2006. Ramirez surprised fans with his strong bat, slick fielding, and speedy feet, which stole more than 50 bases in 2006. It was no surprise, then, that Ramirez signed the team's richest contract ($70 million for 6 years) to date in 2008.

STATS

Marlins seasons: 2006–present

Height: 6-foot-3

Weight: 220

• 3-time All-Star

• 2008 NL leader in runs (125)

• 196 career stolen bases

• .313 career batting average

HANLEY RAMIREZ
SHORTSTOP

FLYING FISH

Through the first weeks of the 2003 season, the Marlins floundered in last place. Then a young pitching powerhouse named Dontrelle "D-Train" Willis arrived on the scene and quickly became a sensation. Fans packed Pro Player Stadium to marvel at the 6-foot-4 Willis's high-kicking windup and blazing fastballs. Jeff Conine also returned, to the delight of dedicated "Mr. Marlin" fans. The infusion of new blood continued with the hiring of a surprising new manager: tough-talking Jack McKeon, who, at 72, was the oldest skipper in the game.

The 2003 Marlins crept up the NL East ladder as McKeon challenged his team. "I know it's a tall order," he said, "but I believe in miracles." Florida fans came to believe, too, as the team climbed from a 19–29 start all the way to a 91–71 finish. On September 26, 2003, the club clinched the NL Wild Card in a stirring 4–3 win over the Mets, with pitcher Carl Pavano collecting the win and Ugueth "Oogie" Urbina recording the save. In doing so, the Marlins became just the ninth team in major-league history to come from 10 or more games under .500 during a season to make the playoffs.

LEFT FIELDER · CLIFF FLOYD

Cliff Floyd was a natural athlete. A star from the day he picked up a baseball bat, he was also a gifted football and basketball player in high school. The tall and powerful outfielder read pitchers well and was speedy enough to frequently take an extra base. Although injured during the Marlins' 1997 World Series win, Floyd was the first one out of the dugout to celebrate when shortstop Edgar Renteria ended Game 7 with an 11th-inning single. When healthy and manning his post in left field, Floyd used his long arms and loping stride to snag many balls that initially seemed to be uncatchable.

CLIFF FLOYD
LEFT FIELDER

STATS

Marlins seasons: 1997–2002

Height: 6-foot-5

Weight: 230

- 2001 All-Star
- 2-time Marlins team MVP
- 865 career RBI
- 233 career HR

INSTANT REPLAY

Although the National Football League adopted its current instant replay rules in 1999, Major League Baseball had no such review policy in place when Marlins outfielder Cliff Floyd hit a ball to the top of the left-field scoreboard at Joe Robbie Stadium on May 31 of that year. The second base umpire called it a ground rule double, which Floyd immediately contested. The umpire crew chief, Frank Pulli, consulted with the other umps and called it a home run. But when the Cardinals protested, Pulli turned to a television monitor near the Marlins dugout and spent almost five minutes studying the film before reversing his own call and ruling the hit a double. Although the Marlins then contested that, Pulli defended his decision to view the video. "At that moment, I thought it was the proper thing to do," he told reporters after the game. But the next day, league officials disagreed, stating, "use of video replay is not an acceptable practice." In 2008, Major League Baseball instituted an instant replay policy, which allowed certain hits to be reviewed on video. After umpires made several bad calls during the 2010 playoffs, many fans began calling for an expansion of instant replay situations.

MARLINS

JOSH BECKETT

A week later, the Marlins defeated the Giants 7–6 in Game 4 of the NLDS, winning the series three games to one. The final contest ended with a flourish, as a Conine throw to home with two outs in the ninth inning led to a home-plate collision between Marlins catcher Rodriguez and Giants first baseman J. T. Snow; the play marked the first time in major-league history that a playoff series ended with the tying run being thrown out at home plate. The Fighting Fish continued to fly high as they then beat the Chicago Cubs in Games 1, 5, and 6 of the NLCS. Rising young pitcher Josh Beckett took the mound for Game 7 and topped the Cubs in a 9–6 comeback victory at Chicago's Wrigley Field to seal the pennant. Against all odds, the Marlins found themselves returning to the World Series.

The 2003 World Series, Major League Baseball's 100th, was an intriguing matchup that pitted the legendary New York Yankees against the underdog, 11-year-old Marlins. The Florida team entered Yankee Stadium and stole Game 1 by a 3–2 score. The Yankees won the next two, but in Game 4 back in Miami, Florida shortstop Alex Gonzalez homered deep to left field in the 12th inning to win the game and even the series. In Game 5, Penny allowed just two Yankees runs over seven innings to

Although he would later be a bigger star in Boston, Josh Beckett was a reliable hurler for Florida, notching 152 strikeouts in both 2003 and 2004.

give Florida a 6–4 win. The Marlins were just one win away.

Florida began Game 6 with Beckett on the hill. A superstitious pitcher who took pains never to touch the white line on his way to the pitcher's mound and back, Beckett was irked by the media's constant reminders of the Yankees' unmatched championship tradition. "All I knew," said Beckett before the game, "was that we were going to get World Series rings on opening day next season."

With Beckett and Yankees left-hander Andy Pettitte locked in a classic pitchers' duel, something had to give. And something did: Castillo's 0-for-14 batting slump. "Baseball is highs and lows," the second baseman later explained. "I was pretty low, but every game, every at bat is another chance." The Marlins finally scratched out a run in the fifth inning when Castillo slapped a Pettitte offering to right field. Yankees outfielder Karim Garcia charged and made a strong throw home, but Gonzalez—running hard from second base—made a crafty slide, wiggling away from catcher Jorge Posada's swipe tag and brushing his left hand across the plate to give the Marlins a 1–0 lead. Florida added a second run an inning later.

Beckett held off the Yankees through eight innings and then worked a swift ninth, ending the game by scooping up a chopped grounder

CENTER FIELDER · PRESTON WILSON

Preston Wilson was both smart and talented. Valedictorian of his high school class in Bamberg, South Carolina, he broke into the big leagues with the New York Mets at age 23. He soon demonstrated superior arm strength and throwing accuracy from center field and showed that he could catch up with even the speediest fastball at the plate. Wilson wielded a big bat, was able to rip hits to all parts of the field, and had enough speed to post 3 seasons of 20-plus stolen bases. The center fielder perhaps came by his talent naturally, as he was the nephew and stepson of former Mets outfielder Mookie Wilson.

STATS

Marlins seasons: 1999–2002

Height: 6-foot-2

Weight: 193

• 2003 All-Star

• 124 career stolen bases

• 1992 *Baseball America*'s High School Player of the Year

• 2003 NL leader in RBI (141)

PRESTON WILSON
CENTER FIELDER

FLORIDA MARLINS

down the first-base line and tagging out Posada. As Rodriguez flung his face mask skyward in celebration, Beckett became the first pitcher since Minnesota Twins hurler Jack Morris in 1991 to toss a complete-game shutout in a deciding World Series game. The young Florida Marlins, with a 2–0 win over the Yankees, had just achieved one of the biggest upsets in World Series history.

FEELING THE HEAT

I t was the Marlins who were upset the following season. Pavano and Armando Benitez both pitched their way onto the All-Star team, where they were joined by veteran third baseman Mike Lowell and slugging right fielder Miguel Cabrera. But although that core group of players led the team to just its third winning effort ever, Florida ended the season 13 games behind the division-leading Braves and 9 games behind the Houston Astros in the race for the NL Wild Card berth.

The Marlins started the 2005 season with newly signed slugger Carlos Delgado at first base. Delgado gave the club a surge in power at

CARLOS DELGADO

the plate, and his arrival prompted some observers to predict a first-place finish for Florida. The Marlins jumped into the season with a 9–0 win on opening day and were among the division leaders with a 44–42 record at the All-Star break. The team seemed poised to return to the playoffs in September, but it then lost 12 of 14 games to finish the season in third place with a record of 83–79. Following the last game, McKeon announced his retirement and was replaced by former Yankees bench coach Joe Girardi.

HURRICANE CONDITIONS

The Marlins were playing the Mets in New York City on September 3, 2004, when they heard that Hurricane Frances would be canceling their weekend series against the Chicago Cubs in Miami. Although Frances had weakened to a Category 2 storm, it was expected to make landfall in southern Florida the next day, bringing torrential rains and dangerous winds with it, and league officials had decided that the Marlins' games against the Cubs should be postponed until later in the month. Although the players were disappointed not to be playing, they weren't entirely surprised; games had been cancelled or postponed due to hurricanes heading toward the Miami area three other times since 1993. And like everyone else in the region, they were more concerned about keeping people safe than gaining ground in the Wild Card race against the Cubs, who had a three-game lead at that point. Many of the players and coaches had homes in the path of the storm and were eager to move their families farther inland, where they would be safe. "You have to make sure everyone is okay," said Marlins third baseman Mike Lowell. "In the scope of things, [the games] are not that important."

RIGHT FIELDER · GARY SHEFFIELD

Gary Sheffield wasn't entirely happy about being traded from the San Diego Padres to the Marlins in June 1993. But when Florida offered the slugger a 4-year contract worth more than $32 million, his attitude changed. Sheffield rewrote the Marlins' record books in 1996, his fourth season with the club, blasting 42 home runs, batting .314, and scoring 118 runs—all despite being walked 142 times. "The Sheff" slammed three big hits in Game 3 while leading the Marlins to their 1997 World Series win. He was among the game's most recognizable batters, due largely to his dramatic bat waggle while awaiting pitches.

GARY SHEFFIELD
RIGHT FIELDER
FLORIDA MARLINS

STATS

Marlins seasons: 1993–98

Height: 5-foot-11

Weight: 190

• .292 career BA

• 509 career HR

• 9-time All-Star

• 2,689 career hits

MANAGER · JACK McKEON

Jack McKeon joined the Marlins in 2003 at age 72—but his age had no impact on his enthusiasm for Florida's team. Under his leadership, the Marlins improbably snagged a World Series win that year, which made him the oldest manager to claim the championship. McKeon had earned the nickname "Trader Jack" in his early managerial days due to his tendency to trade players frequently. Prior to managing, he played catcher for the Pittsburgh Pirates organization in the late 1940s but never made it to the major leagues. "I was the only player to hit three ways: left, right, and seldom," he once quipped.

STATS

Marlins seasons as manager:
  2003–05

Managerial record: 1,011–940

World Series championship: 2003

JACK McKEON
MANAGER

When the Marlins also decided to part ways with such World Series heroes as Gonzalez and Castillo before the 2006 season, it seemed that Florida was in rebuilding mode again. Things looked even bleaker than expected when the 2006 Marlins won just 11 of their first 40 games. But the power of second baseman Dan Uggla, who hit 27 home runs, and the speed of rookie shortstop Hanley Ramirez, who stole 51 bases, as well as the strength of a pitching staff led by Willis and rookies Josh Johnson and Anibal Sanchez, helped the Marlins surge back to a 78–84 finish. It wasn't good enough to get to the playoffs, but the team was encouraged nonetheless. "We believe in each other," Willis said after the season. "That's all it takes."

But it would take more than faith to overcome the injuries that plagued the Marlins in 2007. The pitching staff was hardest hit, as both Johnson and Sanchez underwent season-ending surgery, and Ricky Nolasco threw with a sore elbow all season. Although Willis was healthy, he delivered a subpar effort, notching only 10 wins and compiling a career-high 5.17 earned run average (ERA). The Marlins finished in the NL East cellar with a record of 71–91.

Two of the Florida fans' favorites were missing by the start of the 2008 season, as Willis and Cabrera had been traded to the Detroit Tigers for six young players. But with few expectations placed on the rookie-laden club (12 first-year players put in time during the season, including 7 who made their major-league debuts), the Marlins established an early lead in the NL East and stayed close to the leaders through September. The team finished out of playoff contention, but its 84–77 record—only the fifth winning one in franchise history—was still cause for celebration in Miami.

The fun continued for Florida on opening day 2009, when Ramirez hit a grand slam to help propel the Marlins to a 12–6 win over the Washington Nationals. Florida swept the Nationals on its way to a 14–8 record during the first month of the season. With the aid of left fielder and rookie sensation Chris Coghlan, the Marlins put together their second consecutive winning season and placed second in the division. Although they finished

2003 MARLINS

WILD-CARD LUCK

In 1995, Major League Baseball introduced a new playoff system that included the use of a Wild Card team in each league. This meant that, for the first time, two teams each year would make the playoffs without winning their division. The new format was controversial. Some fans and experts thought the Wild Card weakened baseball by allowing teams with relatively poor records into the postseason, while others countered that the Wild Card would create exciting playoff games and give a greater number of fans hope during the season. The Florida Marlins "lucked out" by gaining the Wild Card entry both times they won the World Series. In 1997, the Marlins won the Wild Card with a 92–70 record and went on to take out the Giants, Braves, and Indians for the title, becoming the first Wild Card team to win it all. In 2003, the Marlins clinched the Wild Card spot with a 91–71 record, and once again, they capitalized on it for a world title. "A Wild Card team has to play hard throughout the season," said Marlins outfielder Jeff Conine in defense of the playoff format. "Wild Card players are hungrier and better prepared going into the postseason."

HANLEY RAMIREZ

Big shortstop Hanley Ramirez quickly became known
as one of the most well-rounded players in the
game, displaying power, speed, and slick fielding.

Chris Coghlan (opposite), the 2009 Rookie of the Year, and Dan Uggla (below), the Marlins' top slugger, helped Florida go 80–82 in 2010.

behind the powerful Philadelphia Phillies both that season and the next, the big bats of Ramirez and young right fielder Mike Stanton gave Marlins fans plenty of reasons for optimism.

In their short history, the Florida Marlins have proven that they know the way to the top. Already, the team has given its fans two electrifying World Series wins—an achievement that some of the oldest teams in the league are still waiting for. Just like sunshine, optimism is rarely in short supply in South Florida. And with today's Fighting Fish battling on, the thrills are likely to keep on coming.

DAN UGGLA

INDEX